English Muffin Recipes

Quick & Easy Appetizers,
Sandwiches, Mini Pizzas, Burgers,
Breakfast, Sweets and More!

English Muffin Recipes
Quick & Easy Appetizers, Sandwiches,
Mini Pizzas, Burgers, Breakfast,
Sweets and More!
©2018

Off the Wall
COOKING

Amazing
Media Works
Print and Digital Publishing
www.AmazingMediaWorks.com

Paperback ISBN: 978-1947676039

Hardcover ISBN: 979-8-89461-024-5

Table of Contents

History of the English Muffin

Most people think the English Muffin must have originated in England, but did you know that it was actually invented in America in 1894? In fact, those across the pond had never even heard of this breakfast staple until the 1990s when it was first exported to the United Kingdom from the USA. The Brits do get some credit, however, since the inventor was a British immigrant— Samuel Bath Thomas— who became a U.S. citizen.

Mr. Thomas first worked in a bread bakery in New York, then later opened his own bakery where he created a "toaster crumpet," a version of the English crumpet that was both flatter and what is now called fork-split. He used a secret process that included griddle baking to create a muffin that was crunchy on the outside and soft on the inside.

Thomas's technique preserved the "nooks and crannies" where all the delectable toppings— butter, jam, cream cheese— congregate and provide a treat for your tongue. True aficionados know you never want to slice an English Muffin with a knife; doing so would ruin all those wonderful air pockets. Instead, you want to us an English Muffin Splitting Tool, which leaves two equal halves with perfectly preserved peaks and valleys.

Thomas eventually opened a second bakery in a different New York neighborhood, and word spread fast. Fine hotels began serving it as a more elegant alternative to toast, and soon thereafter America in general embraced the English Muffin. It is now a mainstay of American breakfast cuisine. Restaurants, award winning chefs and fast food chains have incorporated English Muffins into their menus.

Since those early days, the Thomas brand has been sold numerous times. In 1922, after the death of Samuel Bath Thomas, the family incorporated S.B. Thomas, Inc. In 1926, they registered the "Thomas" trademark. In 1970, the business was acquired by CPC, food conglomerate; in 1998 it was renamed Best Foods (known for its mayonnaise and other spreads). It was recently owned by George Weston Bakeries, an operating unit of George Weston Ltd., which sold it to the U.S. subsidiary of a Mexican baking company, Bimbo Bakeries USA, in early 2009. In addition to the Thomas' brand, Bimbo also owns other well-known brands such as Entenmann's, Ball Park, Oroweat, and Sara Lee.

Poached Eggs

Who doesn't enjoy eggs
covered with eggs?

Poach your eggs
however you like them
and then create these
delicious English muffin dishes!

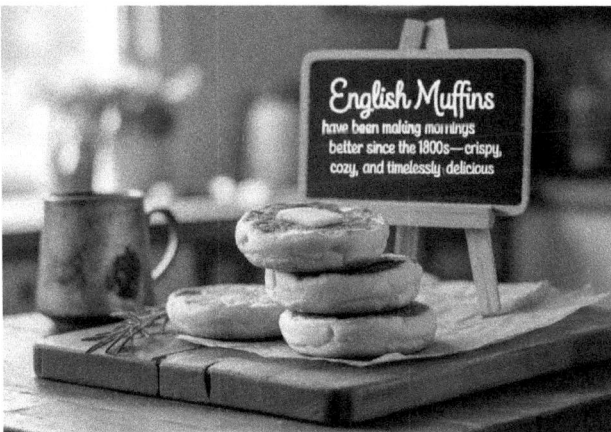

English Muffins
have been making mornings
better since the 1800s—crispy,
cozy, and timelessly delicious

Eggs Benedict with Avocado Sauce

4 medium tomatoes, halved lengthwise

1 teaspoon fine salt

½ teaspoon sugar

4 teaspoons olive oil

2 ripe avocados

¼ cup fresh lime juice

¼ cup water

½ teaspoon black pepper

2 tablespoons finely chopped chives or scallions

4 slices cooked bacon, crumbled

4 English muffins, split

2 tablespoons olive oil

8 large eggs

1. Preheat oven to 500 degrees °F. Arrange tomato halves, cut sides up on a foil lined baking pan. Sprinkle tomatoes with salt, sugar and parsley, then drizzle with olive oil.

2. Roast tomatoes until soft but still intact, 30-40 minutes.

3. In food processor, combine avocados, lime juice, water, olive oil, salt and pepper; process until smooth.

4. In medium bowl, combine avocado sauce; stir in chives or scallions. Separate English muffin halves and brush with olive oil; bake in preheated oven until edges are brown, about 8 minutes.

5. Poach eggs to desired doneness.

6. To assemble, place roasted tomatoes on top of muffins. Top each tomato with an egg, then transfer muffins to 4 plates. Spoon avocado sauce over eggs and sprinkle with crumbled bacon.

You might also like:

- Substitute lemon juice for lime
- Sliced onion rounds

National eggs benedict day is April 16th
But don't wait, you can treat yourself to
delicious eggs benedict any day of the year!

Asian Style Tuna and Poached Egg

1 teaspoon finely chopped red onion

1 teaspoon minced red bell pepper

1 tablespoon frozen green peas, thawed

1 teaspoon minced fresh ginger

1 teaspoon grated carrot

Salt and pepper to taste

1 (5 oz) can solid white Albacore tuna in water, drained and chunked

1 teaspoon freshly squeezed lime juice

¼ teaspoon sriracha chili garlic sauce

2 large fresh eggs

1 English muffin, split and toasted

1. Place the red onion, red bell pepper, peas, ginger, carrots, salt and pepper in a medium bowl. Stir together, then fold in tuna.

2. In a small bowl, whisk the sesame oil, rice vinegar, lIme juice and sriracha. Pour over the tuna mixture and toss gently trying not to break up the tuna.

3. Poach eggs to desired doneness.

4. To serve, top half of an English muffin with half of the tuna mixture, place poached egg on top, sprinkle with the chopped cilantro and black sesame seeds.

Light Eggs Benedict

2 whole wheat English muffins, split	1 teaspoon lemon juice
4 thin slices Canadian bacon	½ teaspoon kosher salt
5 large eggs	Pepper
1 tablespoon butter	3 tablespoons roughly chopped flat leaf parsley
¾ cup low fat Greek yogurt	
1 tablespoon mayonnaise	

1. Preheat oven to 200 °F. Toast English muffins, then transfer to two plates and keep warm in oven.

2. Brown bacon in a small frying pan over medium heat, turning once, about 4

minutes total. Put 1 slice on each muffin half and return to oven. Poach 4 eggs.

3. Melt butter over low heat in a small saucepan. Meanwhile, whisk together yogurt, remaining egg, mayonnaise, lemon juice, and salt in a small bowl. Gradually whisk yogurt mixture into butter and heat until just warmed, whisking often, about 25 seconds (be careful not to overcook the sauce, as it will curdle).

4. Top muffins with poached eggs, pour some sauce over them, serve any extra sauce on the side. Sprinkle with pepper and parsley.

KEEP CALM AND PUT SOME BUTTER ON IT

Smoked Salmon Eggs Benedict with Dill

¼ cup butter, softened

2 tablespoons fresh dill

1 teaspoon lemon zest

1 pinch cayenne pepper

Salt and pepper to taste

1 teaspoon white vinegar

1 pinch salt

4 eggs

2 English muffins, split and toasted

4 oz sliced smoked salmon

4 small fresh dill sprigs

1. Stir butter, dill, lemon zest, cayenne pepper, salt and black pepper in a bowl until combined. Set aside

2. Poach eggs until whites are firm and yoks have thickened.

3. Generously spread each English muffin half with dill butter. Top with a layer of smoked salmon, and a poached egg. Season with cayenne pepper, salt and pepper to taste. Garnish with a dill sprig and serve.

english muffins

Poached Egg Muffin Caprese

1 tablespoon distilled white vinegar	4 (1 ounce) slices mozzarella cheese
2 teaspoons salt	1 tomato thickly sliced
4 eggs	
2 English muffins, split	4 teaspoons pesto
	Salt to taste

1. Poach 4 eggs to desired doneness.

2. Place a slice of mozzarella cheese and thick slice of tomato onto each muffin half and toast until cheese softens, about 5 minutes.

3. Assemble with poached egg on the top of each English muffin. Spoon a teaspoon of pesto sauce onto each egg and sprinkle with salt to taste.

You may also like:

- Use chunky crushed tomatoes instead of fresh
- Swap the pesto for a basil leaf
- Sprinkle with minced garlic

Easy Asparagus Benedict

12 fresh asparagus spears	4 slices Canadian style bacon
4 eggs	1 cup grated Asiago cheese
2 large English muffins, split	½ cup prepared hollandaise sauce

1. Steam asparagus until just tender.

2. Poach eggs to desired doneness.

3. Arrange muffin halves on a baking sheet. Top each with 1 poached egg, 1 slice Canadian bacon, 3 spears asparagus, and ¼ cup Asiago cheese.

4. Broil in preheated oven until cheese is melted and beginning to crisp 2-3 minutes.

5. Heat hollandaise sauce in a saucepan over medium heat until bubbly and hot about 5 minutes. Serve sauce poured over baked muffins.

For the Love of Seafood

The best diet in the world
is the seafood diet - you see food
and you eat it!

Tuna Melts

1 (5 oz) can tuna, drained

4 English muffins, split and toasted

1/3 cup chopped celery

8 slices ripe tomato

2 tablespoons mayonnaise

8 slices cheddar cheese

1. Preheat oven to broil.

2. In a bowl, mix together tuna, celery, mayonnaise and salt.

3. Spread tuna mixture onto the toasted muffin halves and place on a baking sheet. Top each half with a slice of tomato and slice of cheese

4. Broil until cheese is melted, about 3-5 minutes.

You may also like

- Use cheddar and/or Monterey jack cheese
- Add chopped onions

Cheesy Shrimp Wedges

1 (12 oz) package English muffins, split

1 (4.5 oz) can small shrimp, drained

½ cup butter, softened

1 (5 oz) jar processed cheese spread

1 ½ teaspoons mayonnaise

½ teaspoon garlic powder

½ teaspoon seasoned salt

1. In a mixing bowl, combine shrimp, butter, cheese spread, mayonnaise, garlic powder and seasoned salt.

2. Spread the mixture onto muffin halves. Slice each half into 6-8 triangles and place on a cookie sheet.

3. Bake 10 minutes until mixture begins to melt. Serve immediately.

You may also like

- Substitute crab meat for the shrimp
- Top with sharp Cheddar cheese

Salmon and Spinach Scramble

2 tablespoons olive oil

5 large eggs

¼ teaspoon freshly ground black pepper

3 oz thinly sliced smoked salmon, diced

½ cup (4 oz) 1/3 less fat cream cheese, diced

1 cup chopped fresh spinach

3 whole wheat English muffins, split and toasted

1. Heat oil in a medium nonstick skillet over medium heat. Combine eggs and pepper in a medium bowl; stir well with whisk. Pour egg mixture into skillet; cook 30 seconds or until mixture begins to thicken, stirring slowly with wooden spoon.

2. Stir in salmon and cream cheese; cook 30 seconds, smashing cream cheese lumps with spoon. Stir in spinach; cook 2 minutes or until spinach wilts and eggs are cooked, stirring constantly.

3. Top each muffin half with ½ cup egg mixture

You may also like:

- Garnish with chives
- Add sautéed onions
- Top with lemon slices

Chipotle Salmon Burgers

1 tablespoon chopped fresh cilantro

3 tablespoons light mayonnaise

2 tablespoons finely chopped mango

1 tablespoon finely chopped pineapple

1/8 teaspoon finely grated lime rind

1/3 cup chopped green onions

¼ cup chopped fresh cilantro

1 tablespoon finely chopped chipotle chile, canned in adobe sauce.

2 teaspoons fresh lime juice

¼ teaspoon salt

1 (1 ¼ lb) salmon fillet, skinned and cut into 1 inch pieces

4 butter lettuce leaves

4 English muffins, split and toasted

1. Place cilantro, mayonnaise, mango, pineapple and lime rind in a blender and process until slightly chunky. Transfer to a bowl; cover and chill.

2. Place onions, ¼ cup cilantro, chile and juice in a food processor; process until finely chopped. Add salt and fish; pulse 4 ties or until fish is coarsely ground and mixture is well blended.

3. Divide fish mixture into 4 equal portions, shaping each into a 1 inch thick patty. Cover and chill 30 minutes

4. Heat a grill pan over medium-high heat. Coat pan with cooking spray. Add patties to pan; cook 6 minutes on each side or until desired degree of doneness.

5. Top bottom half of each muffin with 1 lettuce leaf and 1 patty. Spread about 1 tablespoon mayonnaise mixture over each patty; place top half of muffin on each serving.

You may also like

- Top with tomato and lettuce
- Add bacon and slice of Cheddar cheese
- Add finely chopped green pepper

Spicy Tuna Sandwiches

1 (5 oz) can tuna, drained	1 tablespoon lemon juice
¼ cup finely chopped celery	½ teaspoon curry powder, or to taste
¼ cup chopped green onion	2 English muffins, split, toasted and buttered
2 tablespoons mayonnaise	4 thin slices Cheddar cheese

1. In a medium bowl, stir together tuna, celery, green onion, mayonnaise, lemon juice and curry powder.

2. Spoon equal amounts onto each English muffin half. Top with a slice of cheese.

3. Place sandwiches on a baking sheet and broil for 2-3 minutes or until cheese is melted and toasty. Serve hot.

You may also like

- Add toasted walnuts or almonds

Mini Pizza Delights

Turn Your English Muffins
into Fast Mini Pizzas.
Enjoy the whole pizza,
or cut your muffin
into 6 pizza style wedges!

Easy Salsa Pizzas

1 whole grain English muffin split	1 strip turkey bacon, chopped
2 teaspoons tomato salsa	2 tablespoons shredded Italian cheese blend

1. Set oven rack about 6 inches from heat source and preheat broiler.

2. Put English muffin halves cut side down onto a baking sheet. Spread 1 teaspoon salsa over each muffin half. Divide bacon between each half and sprinkle enough cheese over the mini pizza to just cover the sauce.

3. Bake under the broiler until the cheese is melted, about 10 minutes.

You may also like:

- Add diced onions or bell peppers

Pineapple Mini Pizzas

½ lb ground Italian sausage

½ teaspoon garlic salt

¼ teaspoon dried oregano

1 cup crushed pineapple, drained

4 English muffins, split

1 (6 oz) can tomato paste

1 (8 oz) package shredded mozzarella cheese

1. Preheat oven to 350 ºf.

2. Brown Italian sausage in a large, deep skillet over medium heat.

3. Drain sausage and mix in garlic salt, oregano and crushed pineapple

4. Place muffins halves on lightly greased baking sheet. Spread with tomato paste, then Italian sausage mixture. Top with mozzarella cheese.

You may also like

- Substitute tomato paste for canned pizza sauce
- Sprinkle with cinnamon

Pepperoni Pizza Muffin Snacks

4 English muffins, split

2 cups shredded mozzarella cheese

½ cup canned or jarred pizza sauce

16 slices pepperoni sausage

1. Preheat oven to 375 degrees °F.

2. Place the English muffin halves cut side up onto a baking sheet.

3. Spoon some of the pizza sauce onto each muffin.

4. Top with mozzarella cheese and pepperoni slices

5. Bake for 10 minutes or until cheese is melted and muffins are browned on the edges.

You may also like

- Toast the muffins prior to adding toppings for extra crunch
- Add a bit of olive oil to the muffin before toppings
- Sprinkle with oregano

Garden Pizza

1/3 cup coarsely shredded carrot

2 tablespoons chopped onion

1/3 cup chopped spinach

1 teaspoon dried Italian seasoning

1 (8 oz) can no salt added tomato sauce

4 English muffins, split and toasted

2 tablespoons finely chopped green bell pepper

1 cup (4 oz) shredded part skim Mozzarella cheese

1. Coat a small nonstick skillet with cooking spray; place over medium heat until hot. Add carrot and onion; sauté 3 minutes. Add spinach; sauté 1 minute. Stir in Italian seasoning and tomato sauce; simmer over medium-low heat 8 minutes or until thickened.

2. Place muffin halves on baking sheet. Spread 1 ½ tablespoons sauce over each, top with bell pepper and cheese. Bake at 400° for 8 minutes or until cheese melts.

Preserve the delectable textural quality of your English muffins by gently splitting with the English Muffin Splitter by Sirius Chef. Using a knife just ruins those nooks and crannies that cradle the butter and jam so nicely.
You know you want one!

Available at
amazon.com

Product #:
B072QBMYLK

JUST ONE MORE ENGLISH MUFFIN, — I PROMISE! —

Scrumptious Sandwiches and Muffin Burgers

Make your burger
an open face sandwich
using just one muffin half,
or top it with the other half
to make it a full sandwich!

South of the Border Cheeseburgers

1 lb ground beef

1 dash hot pepper sauce, or to taste

1 avocado – peeled, pitted and sliced.

3 slices Monterey Jack cheese, cut into 1 inch wide strips

3 jumbo English muffins, split and toasted

3 teaspoons Dijon mustard

1 (4 oz) can diced green chile peppers, drained

1. Mix ground beef with hot pepper sauce, make into 3 patties and cook over medium heat, about 4 minutes.

2. Top each patty with two pieces of cheese. Cover and turn off the heat.

3. Spread bottom half of muffin lightly with Dijon mustard. Layer with avocado, beef and green chilies. Top with the other muffin half.

You may also like

- Add chipotle peppers or garlic powder.

Page 31

Chicken Melt

1 tablespoon butter	1 teaspoon rosemary
1 onion, sliced into thin rings	¼ teaspoon dried thyme
1 teaspoon garlic powder	4 slices Swiss cheese
4 skinless, boneless chicken breasts	4 English muffins, split and toasted

1. Preheat grill for high heat.

2. Sauté onions in butter over medium heat. Sprinkle with garlic powder.

3. Place chicken breast halves on the grill, sprinkle with rosemary and thyme. Cook for about 8 minutes. Turn and continue cooking until juices run clear.

4. Place a slice of cheese on each breast half, top with onions. Cook until cheese starts to melt. Serve on toasted English muffins.

Hawaiian Pork Burgers

1 can (8 oz) crushed pineapple, drained

1/3 cup barbecue sauce

1 tablespoon soy sauce

1 lb ground pork

¼ cup plain dried bread crumbs2 tablespoons minced onion

1 tablespoon minced fresh ginger

1 tablespoon packed light brown sugar

1/8 teaspoon cayenne

1/8 teaspoon salt

4 English muffins, split and toasted

8 large fresh basil leaves

1. Prepare a charcoal or gas grill for medium heat. In a small bowl combine pineapple, barbecue sauce and soy sauce. Set aside.

2. In a medium bowl, combine pork, bread crumbs, onion, ginger, brown sugar, cayenne and salt.

3. Shape mixture into 4 patties. Cook, turning once, until slightly charred and cooked to desired doneness (about 7 minutes for medium).

4. Put each burger on a muffin half. Top each with 2 basil leaves, about 2 tablespoons sauce and the muffin top.

You may also like:

- Slice of Swiss cheese

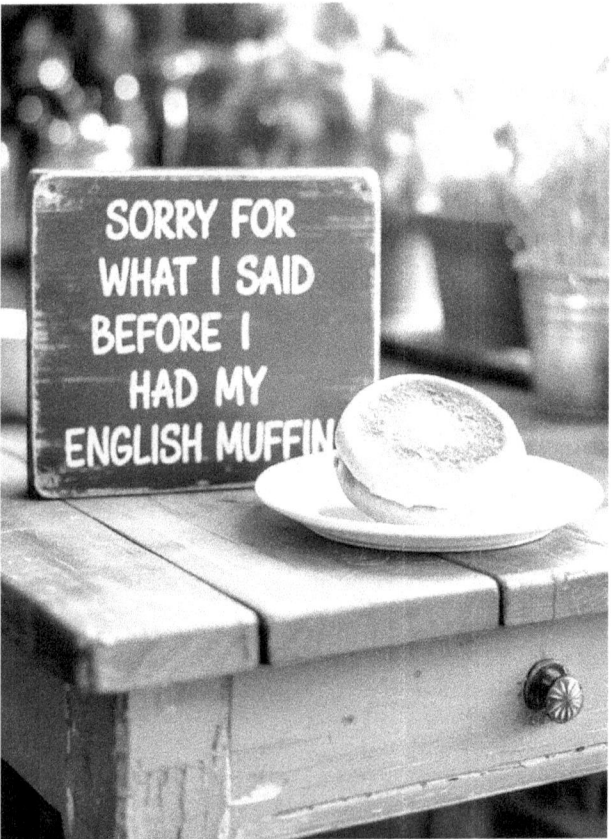

Party Time Pizza Burgers

1 onion, minced

3 stalks celery, minced

4 lbs ground beef

1 (32 oz) bottle ketchup

½ (10.75 oz) can condensed tomato soup

½ (6 oz) can tomato paste

1 ½ teaspoons garlic salt

Salt and pepper to taste

1 ½ (6 oz) can tomato paste

1 ½ tablespoons dried oregano

1 ½ tablespoons white sugar

¼ cup butter, softened

36 English muffins, split

72 slices American cheese, cut into strips

1. Preheat oven to 350 degrees ºf.

2. Place onion and celery into a pot, cover with water and bring to a boil. Simmer until tender, about e minutcs. Drain.

3. Heat a large skillet over medium-high heat; cook and stir beef until it is crumbly and evenly browned, about 5 minutes. Drain and discard grease. Stir in onion mixture,

ketchup, tomato soup, ½ can tomato paste, garlic salt, salt and pepper. Set aside to cool

4. Mix remaining 1 ½ cans tomato paste, oregano, and sugar in a small bowl. Season with salt and pepper.

5. Butter each English muffin half, then spread with tomato paste mixture. Divide ground beef mixture over each muffin half and top with strips of American cheese. Place open-faced sandwiches on large baking sheets.

6. Bake in preheat oven until cheese melts, about 15 minutes.

To Freeze ahead of time: place on baking sheet and freeze. Once frozen wrap each burger in foil or plastic wrap. When ready to eat, place in oven at 350 until heated through, about 20 minutes.

When life throws you a burger... eat it!

Beef Burgers

1 lb ground beef	1 dash Worcestershire sauce
4 soft sun-dried tomatoes, chopped	1 dash hot pepper sauce
2 green onions, finely chopped	Salt & pepper to taste
2 cloves garlic, minced	1 teaspoon vegetable oil
½ green bell pepper, chopped	8 English muffins, split and toasted
3 tablespoons bread crumbs	

1. Mix the beef, sun-dried tomato, green onions, garlic, bell pepper, egg, bread crumbs, Worcestershire sauce, salt and pepper together in a bowl. Form into 8 patties approximately ½ inch thick.

2. Heat the vegetable oil in a skillet over medium-high heat. Cook the burgers in the hot skillet.

3. Serve on toasted English muffins.

You may also like

- Top with tomato and lettuce
- Add bacon and slice of Cheddar cheese
- Add finely chopped green pepper
- Add a dash of liquid smoke to the beef mixture

Egg Salad with Tomato Basil

8 hard boiled eggs, sliced

¼ cup mayonnaise

½ teaspoon Dijon mustard

¼ teaspoon onion powder

1/8 teaspoon salt

Pepper to taste

10 leaves basil, thinly sliced

1 tomato, sliced

4 leaves lettuce

4 English muffins, split and toasted

1. Mix eggs, mayonnaise, Dijon mustard, onion powder, salt and black pepper in a bowl. Fold basil into egg mixture.

2. Arrange tomato slices and lettuce on top of toasted English muffins. Spoon egg mixture over vegetables and serve.

You may also like:

- Season with Dijon mustard
- Add cucumber, pickles or onions

Sandwiches with Tofu

4 green leaf lettuce leaves

4 honey wheat double-fiver English muffins), split and toasted

Tofu Salad

4 tomato slices

Freshly ground black pepper to taste

1. Place 1 lettuce leaf on the bottom half of each English muffin. Layer with 1 tomato slice.

2. Spoon 1/3 cup Tofu salad evenly over each tomato slice; sprinkle with black pepper. Top with remaining muffin halves to make a sandwich.

The secret to Success in life is to eat more English muffins

Breakfast Muffins

Start the day
with a proper breakfast...
and an English muffin!

Breakfast Strata

1 (16 oz) package turkey breakfast sausage

¾ cup chopped green bell pepper

¾ cup bottled roasted red bell pepper, drained

½ cup chopped onion

1 (13 oz) package whole wheat English muffins, split and toasted

2 cups (8 oz) reduced fat shredded sharp Cheddar cheese, divided

4 large eggs

4 large egg whites

1 ½ cups 1% low fat milk

1 teaspoon dry mustard

¼ teaspoon ground red pepper

1. Heat a large nonstick skillet over medium-high heat. Coat pan with cooking spray. Add sausage, green and red peppers and onion. Sauté 9 minutes or until sausage is browned and vegetables are tender. Drain and set aside.

2. Cut muffin halves into quarters and arrange in an 11 x 17 inch baking dish coated with cooking spray. Sprinkle half of

sausage mixture and 1 cup cheese over muffins.

3. Combine eggs, egg whites, milk, mustard and ground red pepper; stir well with a whisk. Pour evenly over mixture in baking dish. Top wit remaining sausage mixture and remaining 1 cup cheese. Cover and chill at least 8 hours.

4. Bake uncovered at 350° for 45 minutes. Let stand 10 minutes before serving.

You may also like:

- A spoonful of peanut butter
- Add chocolate chips

A day without an English muffin is like a day without sunshine.

Golden Onions with Eggs

1 ¼ lbs onions, thinly sliced	1 cup fat-skimmed chicken broth
2 tablespoons butter or margarine	¼ cup all-purpose flour
6 hard-cooked large eggs	1 cup low-fat milk
	4 English muffins, split and toasted

1. Sauté onions in butter until lightly browned.
2. Shell and chop eggs.
3. Mix a little broth with flour to make a smooth paste, then add remaining broth and mix into onion mixture. Add milk and stir over high heat until boiling, then stir about 2 minutes more.
4. Add eggs to sauce and mix well.
5. Spoon sauce onto muffin halves. Salt to taste.

You may also like:

- Sprinkle with parsley
- Add shredded cheddar

Favorite French Toast

2 eggs

½ cup milk

¼ teaspoon salt

½ teaspoon ground nutmeg

3 English muffins with raisins, halved

2 tablespoons butter

1 cup white sugar

1. Mix eggs, milk, salt and nutmeg together with a fork.

2. Let the muffin halves soak on each side in the egg mixture. Spread a layer of sugar on a plate and dip both sides of the bread in the sugar.

3. Melt half the butter in a pan and place two muffin halves in the pan. Cook for 2-3 minutes on each side. Wipe butter from pan, and repeat with remaining slices.

You may also like

- Add cinnamon and vanilla

Classic French Toast

4 large eggs	6 English muffins, split
1 cup nonfat buttermilk	Vegetable cooking spray
2 teaspoons orange zest	1 cup fat-free Greek yogurt
1 teaspoon vanilla extract	2 tablespoons maple syrup

1. Whisk together eggs, buttermilk orange zest and vanilla. Place English muffins in a 13 x 9 inch baking dish, overlapping edged. Pour egg mixture over muffins. Cover and chill 8-12 hours.

2. Remove muffins from remaining liquid, discard remaining liquid.

3. Cook muffins in a large skillet coated with cooking spray over medium-high heat 2-3 minutes on each side or until golden.

4. Stir together yogurt and syrup until well blended. Serve over muffins.

You may also like

- Add toppings such as; chopped fresh strawberries, sliced bananas or chopped fresh nectarines.

Soupy Sauce Egg Muffins

1 (10.5) ounce can condensed cream of chicken soup

1 (10.75 ounce) can milk

8 eggs

8 strips Canadian-style bacon

4 English muffins, split and toasted

1. Split English muffins in half and toast; set aside. In a small saucepan, heat soup and milk over low heat.

2. Place Canadian bacon in a large, deep skillet. Cook over medium high heat until evenly brown. Set aside and keep warm.

3. Add eggs to skillet and cook as desired.

4. Place muffin halves on serving plates. Top with Canadian bacon then eggs. Spoon warm soup over the eggs.

You may also like:

- Sprinkle the top with cheddar cheese
- Add freshly ground pepper
- Substitute grilled chicken for the Canadian bacon

Light Breakfast Sandwich

¾ cup liquid egg whites

½ cup baby spinach leaves

2 whole-wheat English muffins split

2 slices fresh tomato

1. Cook egg whites in a nonstick skillet over medium heat until opaque, about 4 minutes

2. Toast English muffins. Divide cooked egg whites between 2 muffin bottoms. Top with spinach, 1 tomato slice and remaining muffin top.

You may also like:

- Cook eggs in coconut oil for added flavor
- Add a sliced onion ring

I'D GIVE UP ENGLISH MUFFINS, BUT I'M NOT A QUITTER

Delicious Snacks
and Appetizers

English muffins
are your best friend
for creating amazing snacks
and appetizers!

Easy Bruschetta

4 English muffins, split

4 cloves garlic, minced

2 tablespoons butter

1 tablespoon chopped fresh basil

4 large fresh tomatoes, peeled and chopped

8 black olives, pitted and halved

2 tablespoons tomato paste

1 tablespoon olive oil

2 teaspoons lemon juice

1 teaspoon honey

4 slices Mozzarella cheese, halved

Salt & pepper to taste

1. Toast muffin halves under broiler until golden, about 2-3 minutes.

2. Mix garlic, butter and basil together in a small bowl; spread mixture evenly onto each toasted muffin half.

3. Combine tomatoes, olives, and tomato paste in a large bowl; set aside. Whisk together the olive oil, lemon juice, and honey in a small bowl.

4. Spoon some of the tomato mixture onto each muffin, then drizzle the olive oil

mixture over the top. Place a piece of Mozzarella on top and season with salt and pepper.

5. Return muffins to broiler; cook until the cheese has melted, 1-2 minutes. Serve immediately.

You may also like

- Use shredded Mozzarella instead of sliced
- Add a bit of oregano

Apple & Peanut Butter Rounds

½ cup peanut butter

4 English muffins, split and toasted

1 red apple, cored and sliced

¼ cup packed brown sugar

2 tablespoons margarine

¼ teaspoon ground cinnamon

1. Spread 1 tablespoon of peanut butter onto each English muffin half. Top each with a few apple slices.

2. In the microwave, melt together the brown sugar, margarine and cinnamon, stirring frequently until smooth.

3. Drizzle the cinnamon mixture over apple slices.

You may also like:

- Add fresh bananas
- Try with other types of nut butters
- Drizzle with honey

People who love English Muffins are always the Best People!

Sautéed Cherry Tomatoes with Tarragon

1 teaspoon olive oil

¼ cup diced shallots

2 cups halved cherry tomatoes

¼ teaspoon freshly ground black pepper

1/8 teaspoon salt

1 teaspoon chopped fresh tarragon

3 oz thinly sliced part skim Mozzarella cheese

2 English muffins, split and toasted

1. Heat oil in a medium nonstick skillet over medium-high heat. Add shallots and sauté 2 minutes. Add tomatoes, pepper and salt; sauté 2 minutes. Remove from heat; stir in tarragon.

2. Prepare broiler

3. Divide cheese evenly among muffin halves. Place muffins on a baking sheet, and broil 1 minute or until cheese melts. Spoon 1/3 cup tomato mixture over each muffin half. Serve immediately.

Sweet Bananas and Creme

2 tablespoons chocolate-hazelnut spread

2 English muffins, split and toasted

1 banana, sliced

2 tablespoons marshmallow cream

1. Spread 1 tablespoon chocolate-hazelnut spread on 1 half of each English muffin. Layer with banana slices.

2. Spread 1 tablespoon marshmallow cream on the other half.

3. Press both halves together to create a sandwich.

You may also like:

- A spoonful of peanut butter
- Add chocolate chips

Crab Canapes

½ cup butter, softened

1 cup processed cheese sauce

½ teaspoon garlic salt

½ teaspoon seasoning salt

1 (6oz) can crabmeat

6 English muffins, split

1. In a medium mixing bowl, blend butter, cheese, garlic salt, seasoning salt, and crab meat. Spread mixture on split muffins.

2. Cut muffins into 6 pie shaped slices and place on cookie sheet.

3. Bake in preheated 400° oven for 12 minutes.

You may also like:

- Substitute shredded Cheddar for processed cheese sauce
- Add bacon
- Make crab mixture ahead and freeze

Homemade English Muffins

There's no taste like home!

DIY Quick English Muffins

1 cup milk

2 tablespoons white sugar

1 (.25 oz) package active dry yeast

1 cup warm water (110 degrees F)

¼ cup melted shortening

6 cups all purpose flour

1 teaspoon salt

2 tablespoons cornmeal, or as needed

1. Warm the milk in a small saucepan until it bubbles, remove from heat. Mix in sugar, stir until dissolved. Let cool until lukewarm. In a small bowl, dissolve yeast in warm water. Let stand until creamy, about 10 minutes.

2. In a large bowl, combine milk, yeast mixture, shortening and 3 cups flour. Beat until smooth. Add salt and rest of flour, or enough to make a soft dough. Knead. Place in greased bowl, cover, and let rise.

3. Punch down. Roll out to about 1/2 inch thick. Cut rounds with biscuit cutter or

drinking glass. Sprinkle waxed paper with cornmeal and set the rounds on this to rise. Dust tops of muffins with cornmeal. Cover and let rise 1/2 hour.

4. Heat greased griddle. Cook muffins on griddle about 10 minutes on each side on medium heat. Keep baked muffins in a warm oven until all have been cooked. Allow to cool and place in plastic bags for storage.

You may also like

- Add raisins or cranberries
- Season batter with cinnamon or orange zest

Homemade English Muffins

¼ cup almond or cashew flour

1 tablespoon coconut flour

¼ teaspoon baking soda

1/8 teaspoon kosher salt

1 egg

½ tablespoon melted coconut oil

2 tablespoons water

1. Whisk together the dry ingredients in a small bowl.

2. Add the remaining wet ingredients and whisk again until fully incorporated.

3. Transfer the mixture into a greased microwave safe ramekin. Microwave 2 minutes.

4. Remove from ramekin, slice the muffin in half and toast for 2-3 minutes in a toaster oven. Serve with softened butter.

For the cinnamon raisin option add the following to the regular option above:

- ¼ teaspoon cinnamon
- ½ tablespoon maple syrup
- 1 ½ tablespoons golden raisins

Grain-Free English Muffins

1 1/3 cup blanched almond flour	3 extra large organic eggs, or 4 large
¼ cup coconut flour	½ cup water
1 teaspoon salt	1 tablespoon honey
1 teaspoon baking soda	

1 tablespoon fat of choice (olive oil, ghee, butter, coconut oil, bacon grease)

1. Preheat oven to 400F, and grease a 6 1/2 cup ramekins.

2. Mix together the dry ingredients, then stir or cut in your fat of choice.

3. Whisk together eggs, water and honey. Then mix into the dry ingredients (if you are in a rush you can also just throw it all in together; the batter is very forgiving).

4. Divide the batter evenly between the ramekins, and bake for 15-20 minutes until firm. Allow to cool for at least 5 minutes before topping or eating.

english muffins

Paleo and Vegan English Muffins

2 tablespoons almond flour

1 large egg or 2 egg whites

½ teaspoon baking powder

1-2 tablespoons almond milk

2 tablespoons canned unsweetened pumpkin

Cinnamon

Sea salt

1. Spray a medium microwave safe bowl with cooking spray and add peanut flour and baking powder and mix until combined

2. Add canned pumpkin and 2 egg whites or 1 egg and mix very well until all ingredients are fully incorporated. Add almond milk or other liquid of choice.

3. Add cinnamon and sea salt and put into the microwave for 2-4 minutes, depending on the power

4. Remove from microwave and dust either side generously with gluten-free flour. Allow to cool, slice in half and pop in a toaster. Top as you like.

For the oven option:

Follow as above, but preheat an oven to 350 Fahrenheit and bake for 12-15 minutes, or until golden brown on top and a tooth pick comes out clean (usually about 12 minutes). Grease the oven-safe bowl very well to easily slip out.

Notes: Keep a good eye on the microwave-cooking this for too long will result in a drier muffin. These can be made in batches and frozen for up to 4 weeks.

For the Vegan option:

2 T peanut flour

1/2 tsp baking powder

2 T canned unsweetened pumpkin

1 flax egg (1 T flaxseed meal + 3 T water)

1-2 T almond milk

Cinnamon

english muffins

MY RECIPE: _____

SERVINGS: _____

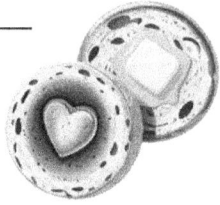

INGREDIENTS:

_____   _____

_____   _____

_____   _____

_____   _____

INSTRUCTIONS:

_____

_____

_____

_____

_____

_____

PREP TIME: _____   COOK TIME: _____

english muffins

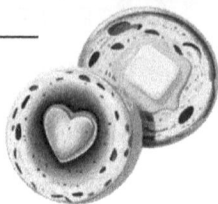

MY RECIPE: _____

SERVINGS: _____

INGREDIENTS:

_____   _____

_____   _____

_____   _____

_____   _____

INSTRUCTIONS:

_____

_____

_____

_____

_____

_____

PREP TIME: _____   COOK TIME: _____

english muffins

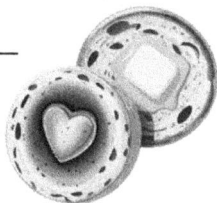

MY RECIPE: _____

SERVINGS: _____

INGREDIENTS:

_____   _____

_____   _____

_____   _____

_____   _____

INSTRUCTIONS:

_____

_____

_____

_____

_____

_____

PREP TIME: _____   COOK TIME: _____

Also by Off the Wall Cooking...

ISBN: 978-1947676244
Amazon: 1947676245

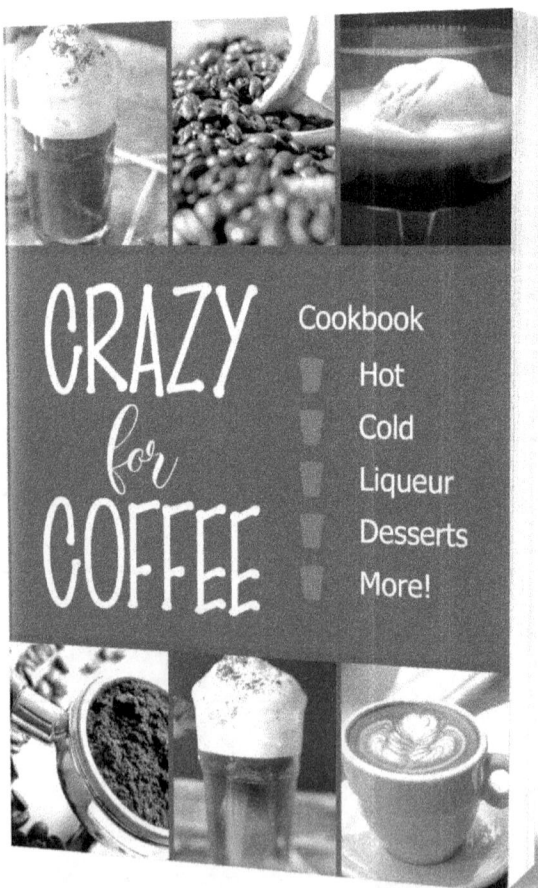

CRAZY
for
COFFEE

Cookbook
Hot
Cold
Liqueur
Desserts
More!

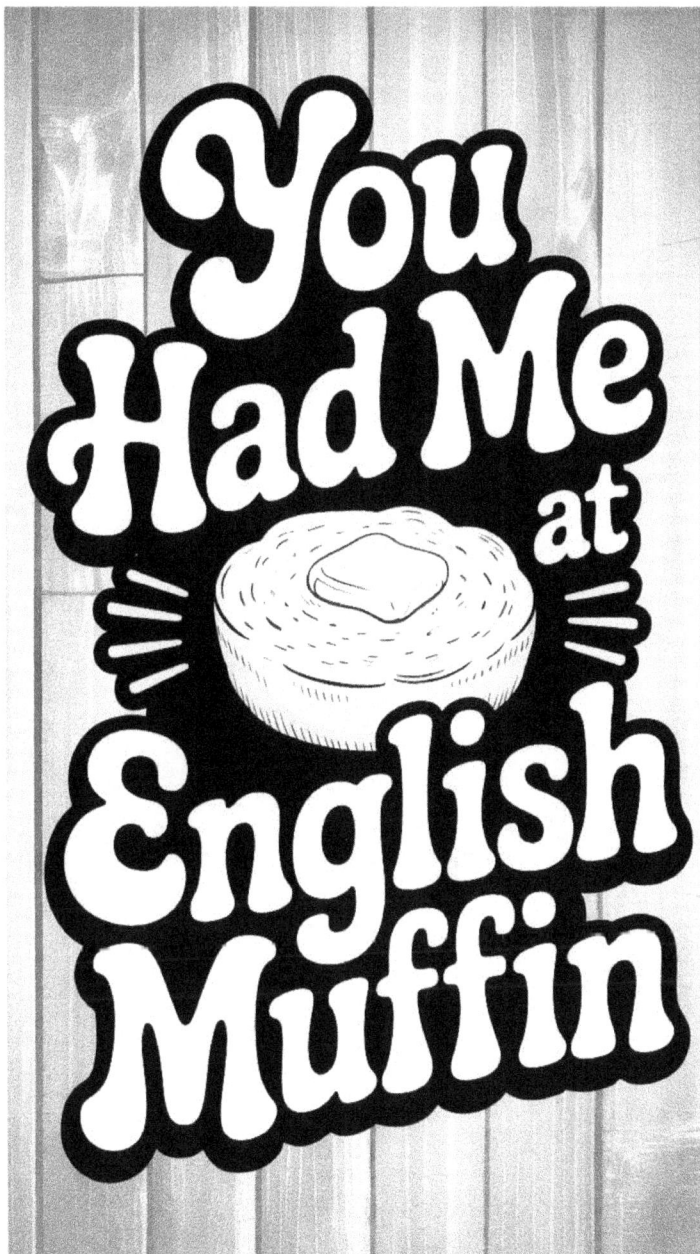

You Had Me at English Muffin

A Note from the Creator

Thank you so much for choosing this book! It's been a joy creating these English Muffin Recipes, and I sincerely hope it brings you as much enjoyment as I had in creating it.

Your support means so much to me! If you could leave a review on Amaz ☆ ☆ ☆ ☆ ☆ it would mean the world. Your feedback helps me grow and connect with more wonderful people like you.

About

Michelle Brubaker is the creator of Off the Wall Cooking. She is also the founder of best-selling activity book brand Puzzle Favorites selling over 100,000 copies worldwide. She resides in the beautiful Pacific Northwest and enjoys creating coloring and puzzle books, as well as teaching entrepreneurs how to build their own successful publishing businesses through her courses and mentoring programs.

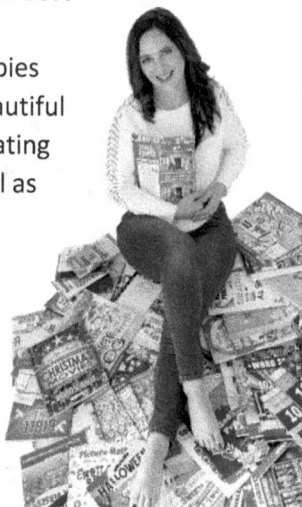

With Heartfelt Thanks...

Michelle Brubaker

✉ hi@michellebrubaker.com

www.ingramcontent.com/pod-product-compliance
Lightning Source LLC
Chambersburg PA
CBHW071843020426
42331CB00007B/1830